THE
LAST
LAUGH
JOURNAL

STEVE & BEKAH
LEGG

THE LAST LAUGH

JOURNAL

*Choosing joy,
one day at a time*

STEVE & BEKAH LEGG

scm

Don't be afraid, for I am with you.
Don't be discouraged, for I am your God.
I will strengthen you and help you.
I will hold you up with my victorious right hand.

(Isaiah 41:10, NLT)

Contents

With a little help from my friends

Writing a book is a little like trying to build IKEA furniture without instructions – fun, but you need all the help you can get, and you sometimes end up with three extra screws and no idea where they were supposed to go.

So here's a huge shoutout to our pals who've been with us through the highs, the lows and the occasional writer's block: Dr Mark Stibbe, Joy Tibbs, Laura Rodger, Tony Vino, Andy Gray, Esther Kotecha, Meggie Legg, Tarn Bright, Andrew Saunders and our Facebook journalling friends. Your insights have shaped this work in ways we could never have imagined.

To our amazing readers, we extend our heartfelt gratitude to you for choosing to purchase this book. In the midst of life's trials, it's important to recognise that joy is a decision we can make every day. It's like ordering a pizza – you must select your toppings wisely. That's the main takeaway I want you to draw from this book.

Even when the road ahead seems daunting and the obstacles insurmountable, we can embrace hope, seek out moments of happiness, and find strength in our resilience. One thing we've learned on our cancer journey, with God's help, is to never underestimate the transformative power of choosing joy. It can illuminate even the darkest of paths.

Hello

In life, we often face challenges that threaten to overshadow the joy and laughter we hold dear. For me and my wife Bekah, that challenge came in the form of devastating news. I was told I had just five months to live as cancer spread through my body. Yet, in the face of this grim prognosis, we made a bold decision: we wouldn't let despair win. Instead, we chose to embrace the life we had left with laughter, joy and gratitude, determined to make every moment count.

In the following pages, you'll embark on a journey alongside us, marked by tears, laughter and stubborn faith. As a speaker, author and entertainer, I'm known for my humour and deep-rooted faith in God, and I refused to let cancer have the final say. Bekah was already digging into what it means to hold on to God in turbulent times, and this season has enabled us to put theory into practice as she's channelled her inner Wonder Woman, with her lasso of truth, showing us all what it truly means to cling to faith in the storm.

We believe the lessons we've learned on this unchosen journey could help anyone, whatever the road you are travelling looks like. When we thought Steve had just months left, it made us think about *what* mattered, *who* mattered and *how* we spent our days. We could probably all do with a bit of that clarity in our lives.

We've written this journal to reflect on the decisions we made in those five months (or twenty-two weeks – hence the twenty-two journal entries). It took real intention to not get lost in grief – caught up in a whirlwind of medical appointments – and inadvertently miss the things that matter most. There are always beautiful things to be found if you look hard enough.

Please allow yourself to travel as quickly or as slowly as you like through these pages, to change the order or skip a step or two. Also, deface the book as much as you like. We've left plenty of space, so you can write on the pages, doodle, draw or do whatever helps... unless you're reading a copy in a library of course. Librarians are usually pretty mild-mannered, but don't ever mess with their books.

So grab a pen and a tissue (trust us, you'll probably need both), and get ready to laugh, cry and maybe even snort a little as you journey with us through our story. We pray that some of what we have learned will nudge and prompt you to think about your own story – that it will help you think about *what* matters, *who* matters and *how* you spend your days. Most of all, we hope you'll find the courage to do something with those thoughts and make the bold decision to be intentional about how you live your life.

It serves as a reminder that even in our darkest moments there is light to be found, and strength is waiting to be unearthed during our deepest struggles.

Our journey is a testament to the resilience of the human spirit and the power of laughter to transcend even the most formidable obstacles. We pray that it will be a life-changing trip for you, too. So hold on tight – it might be a bumpy ride, but we promise it'll be worth it in the end.

STEP 1

Time waits for no one

 Quote from *The Last Laugh*

'How long have I got, Doc? Five months? Five years?'

'More like five months,' the oncologist replied.'

 Pause for thought

I've had an unexpected crash course in the importance of time management recently, and it's been quite an education. My prognosis reminded me that life's too short to spend it twiddling our thumbs. Inspired by my late, great magic and gameshow buddy Paul Daniels, I've adopted a new motto: 'Every second counts.' Because let's face it, when the clock's ticking and you've got a limited supply of seconds left, you've got to make them count like they're going out of style.

Steve's story

If you've read the companion book to this journal, my memoir *The Last Laugh* (available online, in bookshops and in Sue Ryder bargain bins nationwide), you probably think you've got me all figured out. You'll know that before the whole cancer bombshell dropped on my doorstep, life was wonderful. I'd been travelling the world for more than thirty-five years, sharing my faith through a daft blend of magic and comedy. I was the master of laughter (though I say so myself), making crowds roar while secretly giggling at my own jokes.

Then came the sudden news nobody wanted to hear. I had five months to live. That was when I was reminded of something Gandalf said in Tolkien's epic novel *The Lord of the Rings*: 'All we have to decide is what to do with the time that is given to us.'[1] I got the quote framed and displayed in my kitchen, and look at it every time I boil the kettle. I needed to decide what to do with the time given to me. Whether you've had a death sentence or just want to reprioritise your life, it's a salient reminder to us all.

---

[1] J. R. R. Tolkien, *The Fellowship of the Ring*.

Reflecting on ancient wisdom

'Lord, remind me how brief my time on earth will be.

Remind me that my days are numbered –
how fleeting my life is.

You have made my life no longer than the width of my hand.

My entire lifetime is just a moment to you;
at best, each of us is but a breath.'

(Psalm 39:4-5, NLT)

Bekah adds:

It is hard to describe the devastation of news like the prognosis we received: the white noise that builds in your brain, making it hard to concentrate; the awful realisation that you have to tell the children they're going to lose their dad; the horror of realising that the future you had taken for granted is blowing away in the wind, and the unbearable thought that the one you love is going to suffer and be taken away from you.

It was hard to make my mind stay still long enough to focus on anything, but two things crystalised in my mind. I needed to make the most of this time and we needed to share it with our kids.

Something to think about

Imagine you were told you had limited time left.

What feelings do you think would surface?

What, or who, comes first to your mind?

Is there something it would make you want to say or do?

What are your fears?

What are your hopes?

Listen up

Quote from *The Last Laugh*

In my mind, my wife had become the proverbial nag – less of a dripping tap and more of a water cannon. She'd spotted a tiny mark, one that hadn't been there before, and something that couldn't be removed with a good scrub. She asked me to get it checked out, but because it didn't hurt, I left it. Unimpressed by my masculine nonchalance, she kept on at me. Eventually, I agreed.

Pause for thought

Amid the hustle and bustle of everyday life, it's way too easy to ignore the crucial signals that surround us – be they indicators of something to do with our health, mental well-being, business or family matters. It can be like trying to have a quiet conversation at a Metallica gig. You can try, but good luck making yourself heard over the screaming guitars and drum solos. When life gets noisy, sometimes all you need is a little peace and quiet to hear the really important messages from those you love the most.

Steve's Story

I love my wife dearly (a strange name I know, but it does rhyme with Deirdre), and she had been badgering me to see my GP (that rhymes, too). I wouldn't have bothered otherwise; I would have carried on with life, blissfully unaware that something might be wrong. I hadn't realised that nagging is often love in disguise. I'm genuinely grateful that we know now what we're facing and that it's brought us closer together — even if most of our bonding sessions involve hospital snacks, MRI results and the occasional eye roll (not one of the sandwiches on offer at the hospital).

Reflecting on ancient wisdom

Pay attention and turn your ear to the sayings of the wise;

apply your heart to what I teach.

(Proverbs 22:17)

 **Bekah adds:**

The voice we need to listen to isn't always
that of a physical person. In fact, it rarely is
as straightforward as an audible voice, clearly
telling us what to do. Much more often it's a
nagging thought or feeling that won't go away.
And that voice might not be trying to talk to
you about your physical health; it might be to
do with your mental well-being, your spiritual
journey or those you love.

Something to think about

Maybe it's time to block out the trivial and open our ears to the vital. The word 'vital' comes from a word that means 'life'. Sometimes we give far too much attention to the trivial and far too little attention to what's important in life.

Aches and pains, coughs and colds, marks and blemishes are usually perfectly normal, but maybe (as in my case) your body is trying to tell you something.

Listen to your people: Is there something someone keeps saying to you that you've been brushing off?

Is someone you love behaving differently from usual? Do they need you to notice that they're not okay?

Listen to God: Have you noticed something you need to hear right now in a Bible verse, a sermon or a quiet voice in still moments?

No time to lose

🙶 Quote from *The Last Laugh*

When my surgeon came in, I asked, 'Can the operation wait till September?'

Holding my hand, Bekah said, 'Mr Sharma, could you explain to my husband why waiting until September is not a good idea?'

❚❚ Pause for thought

Sometimes we know what really needs to be done, but we put it off anyway. I was worried about letting people down if I cancelled gigs. I'm self-employed, so losing income was also a concern. On top of that, the reality of what I was hearing and the potential pain and weeks of recovery didn't particularly appeal to me. So I naturally wondered about delaying the inevitable for a solid nine months, because why rush into surgery when you can procrastinate like a pro?

Steve's Story

Everyone else knew that time was of the essence, and they made me very aware of that. The penny finally dropped, and I realised we needed to catch this thing before it went any further. There was no time to lose. Faster than you can say 'anaesthesia' I was booked in and on a trolley, heading into the operating theatre.

Reflecting on ancient wisdom

Be very careful, then, how you live – not as unwise but as wise, making the most of every opportunity, because the days are evil.

(Ephesians 5:15-16)

Bekah adds:

Benjamin Franklin famously said: 'Never leave that till tomorrow which you can do today.' But that's easier said than done. I, for one, am amazing at finding mundane jobs to help me put off the big important thing I don't want to face. Sometimes it's the sheer overwhelm of how much there is to do that freezes me in my tracks. When that happens I've learned to start lists – to break those big, scary things into manageable chunks I can prioritise and order and feel able to start attacking.

Something to think about

What needs your attention right now?

☐ Health
☐ Family
☐ Work
☐ Friendship
☐ Faith
☐ Church
☐ Mental well-being

What stops you from acting?

Sometimes what we're avoiding is processing how we feel about a situation or a conversation. There are times when boxing up our emotions is a self-preservation tool that enables us to keep going. Opening the lid is daunting because we're not sure what's going to emerge.

Are there any barriers preventing you from paying attention to those things?

We can't always remove the barriers that are holding us back, but sometimes we can find a way around them. What might you be able to do?

STEP 4

This is me

Pause for thought

When life gives us lemons, some people make lemonade. I prefer to make lemon meringue pie and invite my besties over to share it with me. It didn't happen immediately, but when the news about my diagnosis eventually started to sink in I didn't see it as a death sentence – I knew God was with me and saw it as an opportunity to get busy living and get busy laughing.

Steve's Story

At that moment in the oncologist's office, I was a patient being told that I was a dying man. As we left the building, I had a choice to make about what defined me. Was I just a terminally ill patient? Or was I still Steve — father, husband, magician, funnyman and everything else I had always been? Bekah was adamant that she didn't want me to be defined by the words we'd heard. She changed all her plans to enable, in her words, 'Steve to be Steve' for as long as I was physically able.

Reflecting on ancient wisdom

You have searched me, Lord,
    and you know me.
You know when I sit and when I rise;
    you perceive my thoughts from afar.
You discern my going out and my lying down;
    you are familiar with all my ways.

(Psalm 139:1-3)

Bekah adds:

I don't know what has shaped you in your life, but we are often defined by the roles we play, the parenting we received, or our situation in life. It can feel as if we're playing a part instead of living out our life. Knowing who we are and who we were created to be can take a lifetime, but it starts with intentionally thinking about what matters to us, what motivates us, and what makes us feel really alive.

Something to think about

How does it feel to know that God knows you so completely (see ancient wisdom, p.34) and that he sees beyond what others see?

Ask him to help you see what he sees.

Which roles do you perform in life? It might be helpful to think about what only you can do. For example, only you can be your child's parent or your wife's husband. Maybe there are other unique skills you bring to your community, church or workplace.

- ☐ Family
- ☐ Work
- ☐ Church
- ☐ Community
- ☐ What really matters to you?

Are there any values that you choose, or *could* choose to live your life by? Things like honesty, kindness, respect, loyalty and joy?

What motivates you? What (other than an alarm) gets you out of bed in the morning and helps you make the decisions you make?

What do you wish people knew about you?

When do you feel most alive?

We are family

Quote from *The Last Laugh*

'I had met the perfect woman for me. She was, and is, everything I could ever want: beautiful, clever, funny and kind, and most importantly she loves God. She also loves me and my girls. That's not an easy combo to find.'

Pause for thought

Relationships may not define us, but they matter. One of the greatest blessings of our journey has been strengthening bonds with our family – our five daughters. One of them said they wished I could talk about my emotions more with them (to be honest I don't know how I feel about that). Cue the awkward silence and panicked sweating, because let's face it, emotional vulnerability isn't exactly my strong suit. My strong suit is barbecues and loud shirts. But it challenged me to spend more time trying to make sure that each of our girls feels known, loved and valued in the ways I know how, even if I'm not always great at saying the right thing.

Steve's Story

We're a blended family, and although we have recently gone through the blender of trauma, we are truly blessed. Our story began like a cheesy rom-com: two strangers (with young daughters in tow) meet on holiday in France, fall in love faster than you can say 'croissant' and marry the following year on the only sunny day in August.

We tied the knot in front of God, friends and family, but most importantly in front of our five girls. This celebration was about all of us, and was wonderful — or as they say in the land of berets, Beaujolais and baguettes, 'La vie est belle!'

Reflecting on ancient wisdom

'My command is this: love each other as I have loved you. Greater love has no one than this: to lay down one's life for one's friends. You are my friends if you do what I command.'

(John 15:12-14)

 **Bekah adds:**

For some of us, family isn't about blood relationship, it's about friendship and the community we have created around us. A dear friend of ours, Tarn, often refers to her 'family of choice' — the friends she has chosen to do life with, who have become her family — of which we are delighted to be a part. Sometimes the people who share our DNA aren't a safe space, and pursuing those relationships may not be a good idea. Instead, we may need to let them go. Sharing lives and sharing DNA aren't always the same thing. It is good to stop and take an audit of the people who matter to us, whoever they are, and to make sure we're bringing what we want to bring to the relationship.

 **Something to think about**

Draw your family tree (this may only include your 'family of choice').

How sure are you that each person on your tree knows how you feel about them?

Some of the stories that stuck with me from the tragedy of 9/11 were from men and women who, realising they had limited time, left voice messages for their loved ones, telling them they loved them. What would you want your loved ones to hear and know if you had to leave them a last message?

What can you do over the next few weeks to build in quality time and conversations with those you love, and those who make you feel loved?

STEP 6
I'll be there for you

❝❝ Quote from *The Last Laugh*

We started to ask each other some big questions: Who do we want to see? Who do we *not* want to see? What is important? And more critically, *who* is important.

❚❚ Pause for thought

In the early days of learning to get busy living, we were inundated with kindness and friendship. But between all the hugs, get-well cards and homemade lasagnes, we realised if we weren't careful, we would end up spending so long seeing all the people who wished us well that we'd never see our girls, rest or have time to work off the copious amounts of pasta in bechamel sauce. It's a nice problem to have, I know, but it made us think through our friendships: who we wanted to make time for, and who we would graciously turn down.

Steve's Story

We need to think this through in everyday life, too. We can't be everything to everyone; we need to know who our friends are. Our friend Ems Hancock talked to us about spending time with 'radiators' and 'waterfalls'. Radiators are those you can just sit and be around, without needing to do or say very much. They are warm and comfortable, like a radiator. Waterfalls are people who energise you. Maybe they're inspirational, fun or bring out the best in you. She explained that there is a third category, too: drains. They do what it says on the tin: they drain you. That doesn't mean you should never spend time with drains. But be aware of who they are and how much capacity you have for being drained. It's not healthy to run on fumes — unless you're driving a Tesla, in which case, carry on.

Reflecting on ancient wisdom

Share each other's burdens, and in this way obey the law of Christ.

(Galatians 6:2, NLT)

Bekah adds:

It can seem a bit cold-blooded to label your friends like this. I don't think any of us want to find ourselves on someone's drain list, and the reality is we'll all go through seasons of being radiators or waterfalls, and seasons of being drains ourselves. I'm quite sure Steve and I have drawn plenty on other people's resources these last few years and we're very grateful for those who have been there for us. But each of us has a limited capacity on any given day, and if we are to stay healthy ourselves and able to support those we love, we need to be aware of what we can give out, then draw some loving boundaries to stop ourselves from running out.

Something to think about

Which people are important in your life and why?

How much capacity do you have to give out right now?

How can you build in enough time for those who bring you joy and energise you?

Are there places or situations where you can be a waterfall for someone?

Where can you be a radiator, a safe place to just be?

Where might you be able to be a drain? It's okay to lean in on people. Choosing safe people to hold and hear you in dark moments is really important.

Do you need to make any changes to your social habits?

How can you do this kindly?

STEP 7

Keep the faith

Quote from *The Last Laugh*

Bekah was preaching at our church one Sunday. She confessed, 'I don't know what the future holds. I don't know what the test results are going to be, but I know this: God is good. All the time. And it will be okay. It might not be the okay I would choose, but God will still be good, and it will still be okay.'

Pause for thought

This kind of peace doesn't come from a quick prayer or the wave of a magic wand. It comes from a lifetime of learning to live in God's kingdom, in the presence of the King, and not just 'day visits' for a couple of hours on a Sunday.

Steve's Story

A few days after receiving my prognosis, we drove to Norfolk because nothing quite says 'live as if there's no tomorrow' like a weekend getaway to Norwich. I was doing some shows there and spoke at a church on the Sunday morning. My friend Nick, the pastor, told me to say whatever I wanted at the end. I thought long and hard. It wasn't the most profound thing I'd ever said. It was simply this: 'Just do it. Crack on. Don't put stuff off.'

Reflecting on ancient wisdom

I know how to live on almost nothing or with everything. I have learned the secret of living in every situation, whether it is with a full stomach or empty, with plenty or little. For I can do everything through Christ, who gives me strength.

(Philippians 4:12-13, NLT)

Bekah adds:

When I worked as a church leader, I had the privilege of visiting a member of our congregation in hospital. Colin was an incredible man, one of those church statesmen who just carried a sense of wisdom and experience. But he was dying. He'd been diagnosed with motor neurone disease and had been given a matter of weeks to live. He was lying on a hospital bed with a mask over his face to help him breathe.

Talking wasn't easy, but he asked me to read Philippians 4 to him. When I'd finished, he said, 'I always used to envy Paul's contentment. I didn't understand it, but now, lying here, I finally do. You see, it's just Jesus. Jesus is enough. I don't need anything else.'

It was one of the most profoundly moving and challenging things I'd ever heard. I so want to be able to share in that understanding and know what it means to be content in everything.

Something to think about

When we follow Jesus we gain citizenship of his kingdom, but some of us don't take up residency there. It's like we hedge our bets and keep dual citizenship, holding on to two passports.

Where do you feel you have made your home?

Learning to live in the kingdom requires time spent with the King. How do you choose to consciously spend time with Jesus?

Are there other things you'd like to do to build that relationship?

Spend five minutes in quietness, focusing your thoughts on Jesus. If this all sounds a bit new, you might find the listening prayer exercise on the next page helpful:

Find somewhere comfortable to sit and spend time with God. Close your eyes and go, in your mind, to somewhere you feel safe.

- Where is this place?
- Ask God to meet you there.
- Can you see him, or do you just know he is there?

Take some time to talk with him and ask him these questions:

- What do you think of me, and why?
- What grieves you, and why?
- What excites you, and why?
- If you could take me anywhere, where would it be, and why?
- Is there something you'd like me to leave behind, and why?
- If you had a question for me, what would it be, and why?

STEP 8 · Never say never

Quote from *The Last Laugh*

One mate didn't get in touch at all, then one day Bekah bumped into him at a garden centre. He said, 'I keep meaning to message Steve, but I don't know what to say. This morning I almost asked him how he was. But that's just such a stupid question!'

Pause for thought

There are some things we didn't mention in the book, because the stories weren't just ours to tell. These are stories of relationships we have lost or that have fractured over the years. Some simply with the passing of seasons. You know the sort of thing – out of sight, out of mind. Others have been damaged through misunderstandings and hurt. Healing old wounds and restoring relationships before it is too late has mattered to us.

Steve's Story

Elton John is a man who knows a thing or two about flamboyant outfits and the struggle of saying sorry — because let's face it, 'Sorry Seems to Be the Hardest Word' isn't just a catchy song title, it's a universal truth. But life is too short for grudges and awkward silences, and recently I've been thinking a whole lot more about putting things right wherever I can. So, as a couple, where we have been able — and where it's been appropriate — we have tried to reach out to people and make amends. Because 'Saturday Night's Alright for Fighting', but by Sunday 'Don't Go Breaking My Heart'. I'll stop there, but hopefully you get my point.

Reflecting on ancient wisdom

If it is possible, as far as it depends on you, live at peace with everyone.

(Romans 12:18)

Bekah adds:

Healing a broken relationship isn't always possible, and frankly it isn't always safe. We don't need to restore every relationship. Sometimes maintaining a healthy distance is important. But where we have wronged someone, or where there has been a misunderstanding that we can clear up, it can be incredibly healing.

Something to think about

Twelve-step programmes are a form of therapy that give those struggling with addiction a set of twelve clear steps towards recovery. Participants are encouraged to make a list of those they have wronged, and then to do whatever is within their power to make amends, where that won't bring more pain to the person.

What emotions does the idea of making a list like this provoke in you?

Who do you think you might need to restore your relationship with?

What can you do as a next step in the relationships you would like to restore?

Are there any relationships it would be unwise to try to restore?

If someone isn't safe to talk to, you might like to write an 'unsent letter'. This is a therapeutic tool often used to express emotions, thoughts or messages that the writer chooses not to send. The very writing of the letter can help individuals process feelings, gain clarity or find closure in a private and really helpful way.

STEP 9

Don't worry, be happy

Quote from *The Last Laugh*

With Christmas coming, and my income disappearing, Bekah was worried about how we would manage. We don't have financial reserves; we've always lived one month to the next and trusted God to provide. That approach was being put to the test.

Pause for thought

Part of the decision to get busy living is understanding that worry is like sitting on a roundabout. It gives you something to do, but it doesn't get you anywhere, and can make you dizzy. Don't let your worries steal your life away. It's much better to sit in the driver's seat.

Steve's Story

God was not going to let me down. He never has. I've lived for the last thirty-five years without a regular salary or income, so I genuinely wasn't unduly worried when I had to cancel a load of work. I was self-employed and suddenly became self-unemployed. Yet before we even had time to think about the shortfall, a cheque came in from someone who knew nothing about the cancer, and it covered all my lost income. Just like that. Within a couple of days, more arrived. God was very good (he always is).

Reflecting on ancient wisdom

'Therefore I tell you, do not worry about your life, what you will eat or drink; or about your body, what you will wear. Is not life more than food, and the body more than clothes?'

(Matthew 6:25)

Bekah adds:

I am a middle-of-the-night worrier. During the day I can busy my mind with other things, but at night my anxieties can come back to haunt me. Steve has an extraordinary ability to decide not to worry about things. But he has learned, over the years, that telling me not to worry isn't generally well received or perceived as useful advice. It's just not that easy for us mere mortals. What I have found helpful is writing things down, working out what I can and can't do, and then consciously giving God the things I have no control over.

Something to think about

List the things that are worrying you, big and small:

Things you can do something about	Things that are out of your control

Take time to pray about the second group. Consciously hand those worries over to God and ask him to hold them for you. Maybe visualise leading the people or projects you are worrying about, and then bringing them to Jesus.

Think of some first steps for solving the problems you *can* do something about and maybe diarise them.

Things I *can* do:

-
-
-
-

The Serenity Prayer may help you to invite God into your story:

God, grant me the serenity to accept the things I cannot change, the courage to change the things I can, and the wisdom to know the difference.

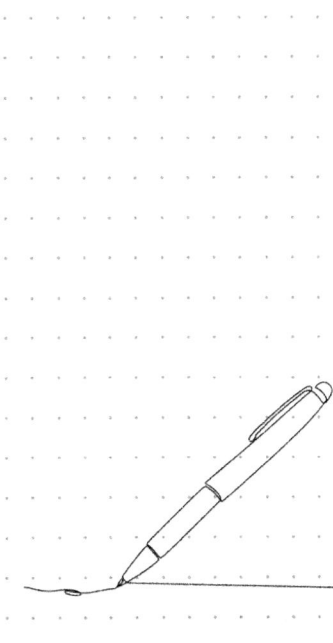

STEP 10

The power of love

Quote from *The Last Laugh*

One time Bekah told our oncologist, 'Steve's skin is very scaly and flaky. I've been rubbing and massaging cream into those areas, but I don't suppose it will make much difference in the scheme of things.'

She replied, 'There's really not much you can do for him, but if that makes you feel you're at least doing something, do it.'

Pause for thought

Sometimes we can't take away the hurts of our loved ones and we can't solve the big problems that concern us in the world. So we need to get on with the little things we can do and leave the big stuff to the professionals. Because sometimes all you need to change the world is a perfectly brewed cup of coffee, a smile and a pot of Nivea.

Steve's Story

Small gestures have certainly made a big difference to me, especially as my main love language is receiving gifts. So, as much as a shoulder massage or back rub is very enjoyable (though my girls were distinctly unimpressed with my appreciative moans), being taken out for lunch, or for an almond croissant and skinny latte (half the calories, all the taste), or for a pint and a pork pie (double the calories and the taste) have been fabulous distractions during various treatments and recovery periods.

I've learned that whether it's gifts, acts of service or just a delicious pastry, it's the little things that make life worth living — one calorie-conscious latte at a time.

Reflecting on ancient wisdom

'We have here only five loaves of bread and two fish,' they answered. 'Bring them here to me,' he said. And he told the people to sit down on the grass. Taking the five loaves and the two fish and looking up to heaven, he gave thanks and broke the loaves. Then he gave them to the disciples, and the disciples gave them to the people.

(Matthew 14:17-19)

Bekah adds:

Shortly after the Covid pandemic I was at a CEO retreat. Coach and consultant Will van der Hart was speaking about the need to build rhythms of rest and downtime. He warned that neither as individuals nor as organisations could we keep running at the pace Covid had demanded. He said that if we did, we would stop being what we had set out to be because we would be stretched too thin and would burn out.

One of the CEOs said, 'But Will, you just don't understand the scale of the need!' He replied, 'When have you ever been able to meet all the needs?' It was quite a challenge in a room full of high-powered people. But it was a good one. We are not required to solve all of the world's problems, or even all of our own family's. We just need to do what we can with what we have, like the little boy with the loaves and fishes, and know that this is enough.

Something to think about

Which problems or issues bother you, but seem too overwhelming to deal with?

Globally...

Locally...

At home...

What are some of the things you *can* do or give?

Take some time to reflect on the offering of the boy in the story, and know that God is pleased with your actions and offerings, too.

STEP 11

It's my life

❝❞ Quote from *The Last Laugh*

I don't want you to think I'm one of those people who pretend the sun is always shining and that there are never any dark skies. That's totally unrealistic unless you live in Iceland.

⏸ Pause for thought

It's okay to make plans for the future, for worst-case scenarios. Having had to do those things last-minute in our lowest moments, we would highly advise having these conversations and making plans before they become such high-stakes decisions. You can always change them. And it might calm some of those worries we listed earlier.

Steve's Story

I went through my garage, then sold all the props I didn't use and parted with my entire collection of magic books, though they were surprisingly hard to make disappear. I also visited a hospice to discuss end-of-life care. That, most definitely, did not make it onto my 'Top 1,000 fun things to do' list, though, on the plus side, I did come away with free parking and two-for-one cinema tickets for life. Seriously though, it was probably one of the worst days of my life, discussing whether I wanted to prioritise quantity or quality of life, like I was in an episode of *Squid Game*. I never expected to be having these conversations in my mid-50s.

I then went online and paid for my funeral: a direct cremation plan in my case, but with a cracking thanksgiving service to follow. I chose my favourite songs and asked some pals to do tributes. My friend Jeff agreed to fly across the Atlantic to speak. That's friendship for you. I planned to have cake, coffee and prosecco for everyone afterwards, because if you're going to remember and celebrate, you might as well do it with a glass of bubbly in hand. I'm slightly gutted I can't be there.

We then sorted our wills, and Bekah called the life insurance people. A lovely lady on the end of the phone helped her navigate a road we never wanted to walk. The weight of all these preparations ground us down emotionally and caused many tears, but eventually they were over and done with. The paperwork, the wills and a power of attorney document went into a drawer and we tried to forget about them, hopefully for many years to come.

Reflecting on ancient wisdom

'But don't begin until you count the cost. For who would begin construction of a building without first calculating the cost to see if there is enough money to finish it?'

(Luke 14:28, NLT)

Bekah adds:

Years ago, my Aunty Dorothy visited from America. She came every year. But this year she caught meningitis and ended up in intensive care, desperately ill. My uncle came to stay with us while she was there, and as a family we listened and loved as he had to make devastating decisions about her care. Decisions to allow the doctors to amputate her limbs, one by one, to try to save her life. Decisions he didn't feel confident she'd be pleased with if she ever woke up. It prompted some deep conversations among my family about what we would want and what we would value. It turned out we didn't all feel the same way, so understanding each other's preferences was a really useful insight that may help us in the future.

Something to think about

What could you do now to prepare for later?

- ☐ Set up a savings plan to cover unexpected expenses or just a holiday
- ☐ Organise life/critical illness insurance
- ☐ Make a will
- ☐ Ask a friend to be the guardian of your children in the worst-case scenario
- ☐ Make a plan for medical emergencies, including thoughts about organ donation
- ☐
- ☐
- ☐

I've started writing down important info in my orange notepad, along with all the things I do and the various procedures that currently only exist in my brain. It sits on my desk and I'm jotting things down in it as I think of them. Bekah has had to create a contingency file at work so that if things change and she suddenly needs to take time off for any reason, the team can easily pick up her work. Now her whole team has created an 'in case I get hit by a bus' manual for their job to ease the stress if they go off sick. It has been a really helpful exercise.

What information do you need to store somewhere handy, just in case? Maybe you need a 'just in case the future's not bright' orange notepad, too.

STEP 12

Take it easy

Quote from *The Last Laugh*

In July 2023, we all went on holiday for a week. It was just what we needed – to be together, with no pressure. We had plenty of good food and, best of all, a gorgeous baby granddaughter to keep everyone occupied and delighted.

Pause for thought

We need to know when to stop, and not try to be everything to everyone all the time.

Jesus took time to get away from the crowd, to be alone with his Father, and to rest. His disciples didn't always understand it – they weren't amused when they found him asleep on a boat in a ferocious storm. But Jesus was more than just resting; he was modelling a way, and a rhythm, of life.

How does the idea of resting sound to you?

How easy do you find it to build in a regular day of rest each week? How easy do you find it to say no to requests from people?

Steve's Story

June to August 2023 was our 'summer of joy'. Our friend Debra had set up a JustGiving page to raise funds for us to do all the things we could never have afforded to do otherwise: meals out, time away and more Insta-fun moments than a mini-break with the Kardashians. People were incredibly kind and generous with their gifts, but after six weeks we realised the pace had become somewhat relentless, and that we were losing time to just be, especially with our girls. So I had a word with Kim, Khloé and Kourtney, and explained we were stepping back a bit to make sure we had enough space to enjoy normal family life. Because sometimes the best memories are made at home, in our pyjamas, with a bowl of popcorn and a remote control on hand.

Reflecting on ancient wisdom

Before daybreak the next morning, Jesus got up and went out to an isolated place to pray.

(Mark 1:35, NLT)

Bekah adds:

I come from a strong line of women who 'cope', and at the beginning, in the first few recovery periods, I did. But as Steve began to get better and was back on his feet, I began to collapse into an emotional heap. After months of being everything to everyone, I was spent. I couldn't cope with anything at all.

During our summer of joy I nearly did the same thing again. As Steve wasn't allowed to drive, I became his chauffeur while still running Restored and supporting the family. But fortunately I recognised the warning signs this time and asked for help. Steve now has an amazing little gang of friends — Martin, Steve and another Martin — who have taken on most of the driving to his gigs, and I do my best not to feel guilty about staying at home.

Something to think about

Are there any things you do that you need to lay down for a while?

Are there people you need to say no to?

Is there a way you can build more downtime into your life?

STEP 13

Lean on me

Pause for thought

We live in a world where independence is valued above all things. Asking for help can be beyond many of us and is often seen as a sign of weakness, so I especially love the Bible story (in the gospel of Mark, chapter two) where a bunch of guys haul their paralysed mate through the streets on a stretcher, determined to get him in front of Jesus. The house where Jesus is staying is so packed they can't even make it through the front door. They're not about to give up that easily, though. They start making a hole in the roof to try to get to the miracle man. And it worked. Jesus saw their faith and determination, and healed the man there and then.

Talk about a rooftop rescue mission gone right. Everyone was thrilled... except the guy who owned the house. Sometimes what you need to do is ask some resourceful friends to tear through a roof or two for you.

Steve's Story

I was utterly useless and helpless for months. Being given a bed bath by a cute blonde (my wife, just in case you're wondering) sounds more exciting than it was. Thoughts of intimacy were drowned in the practicalities of recovery and dependency. Being reliant on others for everything from getting dressed to tying your shoelaces is not exactly the stuff of romance novels. But desperate times call for desperate measures. And if that means sacrificing a bit of romance to get through the day in one piece, then so be it. Sometimes all you can do is hold on tight and hope you don't fall off the bed.

Reflecting on ancient wisdom

As they led Jesus away, a man named Simon, who was from Cyrene, happened to be coming in from the countryside. The soldiers seized him and put the cross on him and made him carry it behind Jesus.

(Luke 23:26, NLT)

Bekah adds:

I find it hard to ask for help, but several years ago I was struck by part of the story of Jesus at Easter that I hadn't noticed before. He couldn't carry his cross up the hill. The weight of the wooden cross after the flogging he had received was too much. He staggered, fell and couldn't get back up — not without the help of a stranger. It strangely liberated me to think that if Jesus needed help, then it's okay for me, too.

Something to think about

Take a moment to reflect on Jesus needing help from someone else. Does that change how you feel about him? Does it change how you feel about yourself?

What does the word 'independence' mean to you?

How easy do you find it to ask others for help?

What stops you?

In which areas of your life do you feel you can manage just fine yourself?

How would it feel to lose those strengths?

What are your weaknesses? What can't you do by yourself?

Who do (or could) you ask to help you counter those weaknesses?

STEP 14

Lost for words

People are lovely, but I just want to crack on with stuff and be as normal as possible. I don't want to be asked about my illness all the time. I often thought: *Wouldn't it be great to have a couple of hours or even days when I don't have to think about cancer?*

Pause for thought

People often didn't know what to say to us after we got the news about my cancer spreading, and one of the things we found most helpful was a friend choosing to ask what we needed from them that day: a shoulder to cry on, a problem to solve, an ear to listen, a laugh, some prayer, a distraction, a cup of sugar or the lend of an angle grinder (maybe not the last one as, when it comes to my practical skills around the house, DIY stands for Destroy It Yourself).

This approach was helpful in the face of a difficult diagnosis, but the same approach could be useful in many other situations – in fact, it could apply to almost any conversation when you just don't know what to say.

 ## Steve's Story

People are as diverse as a bag of Skittles, so what we need may change each day. I wanted to forget about cancer. That doesn't mean I've been closed off to the idea of remembering things, but when faced with a tough diagnosis, sometimes all I want to do is be distracted and have a good laugh.

Reflecting on ancient wisdom

He comforts us in all our troubles so that we can comfort others. When they are troubled, we will be able to give them the same comfort God has given us.

(2 Corinthians 1:4, NLT)

 **Bekah adds:**

I had one very tough conversation with a well-meaning stakeholder at work. They were very insistent about the need for me to be 'emotionally honest'. I had come with my work hat on, prepared for a conversation about a policy, not to have a 'deep and meaningful'. It completely threw me and left me feeling quite wobbly. I know that wasn't the intention, but it felt like I wasn't being allowed to choose when and where I was vulnerable, or even who with. Work was a welcome distraction from all that was happening at home, and it was really helpful to keep the two things separate.

Talking about it with one of my colleagues, we realised this was a lesson we could take into the work we do, supporting survivors of domestic abuse. We must never assume we know what another person needs; we must have the humility to ask and then follow their lead.

Something to think about

How do you feel about having frank conversations with friends relating to what you or they might need on a given day?

Think about the people you plan to see this week. What do you need from those people?

What might they need from you?

What do you need from God right now? Take time to turn this into a prayer.

STEP 15

Walking on sunshine

Quote from *The Last Laugh*

My oncologist had told us we could choose one of two things in response to my prognosis: to live dying, or to die living. I was determined to do the latter.

Pause for thought

We decided that spending our life talking about and thinking about what was wrong would only make us sad, so we chose instead to focus on what brought us joy. It's very simple really.

Steve's Story

So there I was, fresh from hearing that my life expectancy was so short it wasn't worth renewing my library card, but I had comedy gigs lined up just days later. At first I didn't think I could make, or even want to make, people laugh. I wasn't able to string many sentences together without my eyes welling up. But this was about more than just doing a show. This was also an opportunity to share my faith in Jesus with hundreds of people. So after a pep talk from some of my speaker and performer buddies, I decided to give it a shot, bounded onto the stage and did my thing. I haven't stopped gigging since, and I've loved it. Who would have thought a cancer diagnosis could reinvigorate a comedy career?

Reflecting on ancient wisdom

And now, dear brothers and sisters, one final thing. Fix your thoughts on what is true, and honourable, and right, and pure, and lovely, and admirable. Think about things that are excellent and worthy of praise.

(Philippians 4:8, NLT)

Bekah adds:

I've had a spiritual director for the last ten years. I meet with her almost every month, which provides me with a chance to reflect, listen to God, and think about where I'm going. I've found it invaluable.

She often asks me insightful questions, but one day she just asked me, 'Bekah, what brings you joy?' I was lost for words, which is a rarity. I realised that, in the busyness of being a mum, working full time and serving in church, I didn't know. I had spent all my time thinking about other people and hadn't stopped to think about myself — what I liked to do and what made me happy.

Something to think about

Take some time to see if you can name what brings you joy.

For our wedding anniversary in August, I bought Steve a box of cards with fifty-two date night ideas. It was partly a defiant stand in the hope that we would have longer than the doctors said, but it also provided some easy ideas of things to do when we needed to cheer ourselves up.

Why not create your own pack of cards so you have them to hand when you need to choose joy?

Options could include:

- Watching a favourite movie, TV show or boxset.
- Playing music you love (really loud).
- Having an early night or a lie-in.
- Going for a walk in the great outdoors.
- Hosting a barbecue.
- Reading a great book or listening to an audiobook.
- Making a jigsaw or playing a board game.
- Laughing along to a comedy podcast.
- Visiting a coffee shop, cafe or restaurant.
- Going to a museum or art gallery.
- Visiting the cinema or theatre.
- Being pampered at a spa day (home or away).
- Running a deep bath and lighting some candles.

- Going on a shopping spree.
- Calling someone on the phone.
- Hanging out with friends.
- Planning something kind for someone else.
- Doing some baking.
- Trying a new type of crafting.
- Playing a sport or going to the gym.
- Having a picnic in the park.
- Stargazing at night.
- Enjoying a bike ride around your town.
- Visiting a zoo or aquarium.
- Taking a dance class together.
- Attending a live comedy show or improv performance.
- Exploring a nearby town you've never been to before.
- Visiting a local farmers' market and cooking a meal with the fresh ingredients.
- Going to a theme park or amusement park for a day of thrills.
- Attending a live sports game.
- Visiting a historical site or landmark.
- Having a themed dinner night where you cook cuisine from a different country.
- Arranging a beach bonfire and watching the sunset with toasted marshmallows.

STEP 16

Thank you for the days

Quote from *The Last Laugh*

We decided to have a season of choosing to find joy in everyday things: birdsong, sunshine and snuggles together on the sofa.

Pause for thought

There's nothing like feeling as if you've lost everything to make you grateful for what you have left. Many of us have so much and just assume that's normal. It's like we've been trained to always want more, and are never satisfied with what we have. Appreciating things and practising gratitude is not just about saying thank you and showing we are grateful – it's part of choosing joy. It's recognising the goodness in our lives, the gifts that we so easily miss in the busyness of life, and learning to be content with what we have. It's a bit like finding money in an old jacket pocket. It's probably not a million bucks, but it's a nice surprise that puts a smile on your face all day long.

Steve's Story

I started doing the very same thing, even when nature called in the wee hours (pun intended), thanking God that I could still stumble my way to the bathroom without tripping over anything or anyone, and that I even had a toilet to stumble to. The more grateful you are, the more amazing things you'll see.

Reflecting on ancient wisdom

Rejoice always, pray continually, give thanks in all circumstances; for this is God's will for you in Christ Jesus.

(1 Thessalonians 5:16-18)

 Bekah adds:

I used to work for Christian child sponsorship charity Compassion, and I had the privilege of visiting some of our projects. One church in western Kenya sticks in my mind. I was blown away by everyone who participated in the service. Each person started their prayer, talk or song with the words, 'I give thanks to the Lord that I woke up this morning.' It was a moment of realisation that in this beautiful part of the world, and in many others, waking up was not taken for granted; it was considered a gift.

I came away feeling so challenged about the things I had taken for granted and didn't appreciate. Privilege and entitlement can steal our joy as we cease to recognise the gifts we are given each day and instead focus on what we don't have.

Something to think about

What things in life do you take for granted?

What do you need to stop and appreciate today?

CREATE A HAPPY JAR

Choose your jar: Select a clean, empty jar with a lid. It can be any size or shape, depending on how much space you have and how often you want to fill it up.

Decorate your jar: Get creative and decorate your jar to make it visually appealing and personal. Or, if you're like Steve, just leave it blank!

Set a routine: Decide how often you want to add to your happy jar. You might choose to do it daily, weekly or just whenever you feel like it.

Capture happy moments: Whenever something positive happens or you feel grateful for something, write it down on a piece of paper. It could be a joyful moment, an achievement, an answer to prayer, a compliment or anything that brings you happiness.

Fold and add: Fold the paper so that your happy moment is written inside and add it to the jar. You can also include the date if you like.

Review and reflect: Over time, your happy jar will fill up with happy memories. Set aside some time periodically to go through the notes and reflect on the positive moments you've experienced.

Celebrate: At the end of the year (or whenever you feel like it), take some time to empty your happy jar and read through all the notes. Celebrate the abundance of joy and gratitude in your life.

STEP 17   Let it out

❝❝ Quote from *The Last Laugh*

It was April 2023 and we'd just heard the news from our oncologist. For the next few days, I was devastated. These were the first tears I had shed. For the very first time, I was forced to face the reality of what was happening to me. Bekah had been in that same place for the past eighteen months. I'd been stoical up to that point, but now I was overwhelmed.

❚❚ Pause for thought

Choosing joy doesn't mean pretending that grief, sadness, pain and anger don't exist. You can't just ignore them or hope they'll magically disappear, like a bad haircut. Acknowledging those emotions is vitally important, as is creating space to feel and name them.

Our youngest, Meggie, has struggled through periods of anxiety and depression, and she often used to cry in the shower before bed.

When she started seeing a therapist, she was given a new perspective on these bathroom tears. Rather than being something she needed to stop, she was told they were a great coping mechanism. Her sobs in the safety of the warm water enabled her to let out how she was feeling and enabled her to go to bed feeling better. Crying it out changed her perspective and helped her enormously.

 Steve's Story

It might seem like a strange thing to say, but my tears and feelings of devastation came as a relief to my wife. You see, we were finally on the same wavelength. For way too long, Bekah had been carrying all the weight, the worry and the girls' emotions, mainly to protect yours truly. But better late than never. Now we're finally on the same page and walking the same path together — even if it's sometimes paved with tears.

Reflecting on ancient wisdom

Blessed are you who hunger now,
  for you will be satisfied.
Blessed are you who weep now,
  for you will laugh.

(Luke 6:21)

Bekah adds:

I've done my fair share of crying in the middle of the night, listening to Steve sleep soundly and imagining a world where I can't do that any more. I've gone through a Christmas wondering if it was our last, putting on a brave face for the rest of the family so they can live free of that fear. I think it was the right thing to do, but I reached a point where I realised I couldn't hold all of this alone.

I started a WhatsApp group with three precious friends, and it became a space where I could drop my fears and my failings, and send up a flare that would escalate things to a call and a hug when it all got too much. They were like lightning rods — protecting me from damage whenever lightning struck. It was a space where I could say the things I didn't want Steve or the children to hear. These lightning rods have grounded and loved me, and kept me going.

Something to think about

Do you have any emotions you're afraid to face?

Do you have a friend who could be your lightning rod?

Bekah used to work on a rape crisis helpline. As part of their training, staff were encouraged to regularly take the time to intentionally 'let it out' and express their emotions at the injustices they had heard. Here are a few suggestions that might help you do this:

- Playing loud music in your car or at home, and shouting about how you feel.
- Walking in the countryside and crying or shouting into the wind.
- Going to the beach and throwing stones to let your anger out.
- Punching a pillow or throwing soft items at a wall.

The main idea is that there is nothing wrong with grief, sadness or anger, but expressing it in a healthy way matters.

Is there a safe space, like your shower or a secluded beach, where you can let those feelings out?

Might you need some professional help to access and release those emotions? If so, these numbers might be helpful:

Campaign Against Living Miserably (CALM) - 0800 58 58 58
Macmillan - 0808 808 00 00
Marie Curie - 0800 090 2309
Premier Lifeline - 0300 111 0101
Samaritans - 116 123
SANEline - 0300 304 7000
Shout - text SHOUT to 85258
The Mix (if you're under 25) - 0808 808 4994

Laughter in the rain

🙶 Quote from *The Last Laugh*

The heavens opened and it tipped down, but my late-night performance at New Wine went down a storm during a storm, with 500 crammed into the venue to enjoy my 'Tricks and Laughs' show, and another 200 turned away. If laughter is great medicine, then making people laugh is like a super drug. I felt almost back to normal.

▐▐ Pause for thought

Tears and laughter don't have to be mutually exclusive, they can coexist in the same moment. Anyone who has been to one of my gigs will know what I mean. Building intentional laugh-out-loud moments into your day is key to choosing joy. It's the ultimate in emotional multitasking.

Steve's Story

Since 1988, I've been living the dream of performing professionally all over the world, and it's been an absolute blast. There's nothing quite like being on stage, sharing the message of hope through Jesus, while weaving together a crazy blend of comedy and magic to bring a smile to people's faces. I feel incredibly blessed to do what I love best every single day. It's like being a superhero, but with less Lycra and extra-special good news. They say laughter is the best medicine unless you're diabetic... then it's insulin.

Reflecting on ancient wisdom

A cheerful heart is good medicine,
but a crushed spirit dries up the bones.

(Proverbs 17:22)

Bekah adds:

I'll never forget our car journey to those first gigs after we had received the five-month news just days earlier. We'd spent the week in tears. I'd completely given up on make-up, and I had no idea how Steve was going to hold it together to perform. We had a three-hour drive before the moment of truth, and we listened to comedy podcasts all the way. They made us laugh, raised our spirits and just did our hearts good.

Something to think about

When did you last laugh so hard that it hurt?

Who makes you laugh?

What's your funniest memory?

Is there something funny you enjoy watching, reading or listening to that you can add to your schedule as a light spot in your day?

Is there someone you can choose to spend time with who will make you laugh?

Silver linings

STEP 19

❝❝ Quote from *The Last Laugh*

As I gradually came off steroids I was sweating profusely, especially under hot stage lights. A few weeks after one gig, where I'd asked the organisers to open all the doors and windows during the show, the minister wrote to me: 'Thanks so much for coming. Just to let you know, a lady was walking past the church with her son. Because the windows and doors were all open, she heard the laughter from inside the building. They came in for your show, and they've been coming to church ever since.'

⏸ Pause for thought

God is a God of fresh starts, redeemed stories and streams in the desert. There are silver linings to be found in the strangest places if you have eyes to see them. While we would never have wished for the events of the last couple of years, we wouldn't wish them away either.

Steve's Story

There are always so many bright moments to be found, even in the most horrible seasons. God has been so good to us. Who would have thought that my steroid sweats could have such a positive impact on that church I visited last summer? It really struck me. I could have stayed home and wallowed in self-pity, but instead I decided to hit the road and keep people laughing — or at least keep them distracted from the fact that I was sweating like Daddy Pig at a hog roast. And in the process, God used my problem with perspiration as an opportunity for a woman and her son to hear the laughter and start coming to church.

Reflecting on ancient wisdom

The Lord is my shepherd, I lack nothing.
   He makes me lie down in green pastures,
he leads me beside quiet waters,
  he refreshes my soul.
He guides me along the right paths
   for his name's sake.
Even though I walk
   through the darkest valley,
I will fear no evil,
   for you are with me;
your rod and your staff,
   they comfort me.

(Psalm 23:1-4)

 **Bekah adds:**

There is so much I wish we hadn't been through this last year, so many tears I'd never have chosen to cry. But there is also so much that has happened that I don't think would have happened otherwise. Steve and I have discovered new depths to our relationship as we have faced these challenges and shared the pain. The same thing has happened with our kids. We've spent more time together and had our first family holiday in nine years. We've learned to appreciate each other in a whole new way.

Something to think about

What are the dark clouds in your life?

Take some time this week to look for silver linings.

Where is Jesus in your story?

Ain't no mountain high enough

STEP 20

Quote from *The Last Laugh*

After hearing the bad news one Saturday afternoon we went to the pub, got out the laptop, went through our diary, and started to ask some big questions about our priorities in the days, weeks and months to come.

Pause for thought

The reality is, your diary is a 'Windows 11' into your priorities. Be prepared to be enlightened and possibly slightly embarrassed by the revelations it holds. Taking some time to work out what you are giving your time to, and to compare this with what you have been thinking about while reading through this journal, will be an interesting exercise – especially if the diary contains no exercise. I wonder if your priorities and what you think of as your priorities match up?

Steve's Story

I don't know about you, but I often struggle with saying no. There have been times when I've gone along with something because I didn't want to hurt someone's feelings. I mean, don't get me wrong, I'm generally Mr Nice Guy. If someone asks me to meet up for a pint or a curry, I'm usually all in. But thanks to my medical situation, I've been granted the ultimate excuse to decline — and let me tell you, it's been liberating.

Reflecting on ancient wisdom

But seek first his kingdom and his righteousness, and all these things will be given to you as well.

(Matthew 6:33)

Bekah adds:

That Saturday afternoon in Norwich looking at the diary was bittersweet. Five months seemed like such a short time to have left together. But it enabled us to think about what was important and cancel things that were in the way of that. We're so grateful to have had more days, months even, than we thought, but we're trying hard to retain the lesson. This year, before work or other things got in the way, we planned our holidays and key dates with the children, friends and church family. They take priority, and we'll work the rest in around them.

Something to think about

What fills your diary?

Who fills your diary?

What emotions does that prompt?

Priorities matter

There is a great illustration that involves a large jar, some rocks, pebbles, gravel and sand. It will all fit in the jar, but only if you fill it in the right order. If you start with the sand, you won't fit the rocks in.

You have to start with the big stuff, the rocks. Then you can drop the pebbles in around them and they'll squeeze into the gaps. Likewise with the gravel, and lastly the sand, which will find its way into the remaining spaces.

This is a great picture of our lives. Work out what the big stuff is and get that in the diary. Everything else will fit around the edges.

What are the rocks, the most important things, in your life?

STEP 21

One day at a time

Pause for thought

Corrie ten Boom was a Dutch watchmaker who worked with her father and siblings to help many Jewish people escape from the Nazis during the Holocaust of the Second World War by hiding them in their home. She was a remarkable Christian and is often quoted as saying, 'Worry does not empty tomorrow of its sorrow, it empties today of its strength.' That's profound.

One of the things we have had to learn is to enjoy today. We can't do too much about tomorrow, but being fully present today with whoever we are with, and doing whatever we have planned or encountered, will bring the most happiness and peace.

It's much easier to be present today when you have already done what you can about tomorrow. The planning we discussed earlier will help with this.

 ## Steve's Story

We decided to get busy living and to choose joy, whatever the future brings. I've chosen to make sure I have the last laugh, even in the face of death. And when that day finally comes, I aim to go out with a bang – and no, not from yet another DIY disaster involving plug sockets (trust me, I've had enough of those), but in a blaze of glory and a cloud of confetti. For now I'm cracking on: writing, podcasting and travelling around the country, sharing my story and, most importantly, the good news of Jesus for as long as I can. After all, why wait for the grand finale when you can have a blast every single day?

Reflecting on ancient wisdom

Refuse to worry about tomorrow, but deal with each challenge that comes your way, one day at a time. Tomorrow will take care of itself.

(Matthew 6:34, TPT)

Bekah adds:

I've had two 'last Christmases' with Steve. I enjoyed the second much more than the first, even though it was more likely to be the actual last. It's partly about the timing. Before Christmas 2022 we'd just received the news that Steve's cancer had spread, and I kept getting caught by waves of sadness that this might be the end. It wasn't, but I lost a lot of enjoyment thinking about it. Christmas 2023 was a different season altogether. Some of that was because the latest scans had provided good news, but it also came down to the fact that I'd learned to just enjoy today; to grab the gift of an extra Christmas with both hands, and celebrate it with the people I loved most rather than spending my time worrying about what might come next year.

Something to think about

What do you have planned for today that you are looking forward to?

What do you want to achieve today?

Who do you want to love today?

How do you want to leave people feeling after they have spent time with you?

Is there anything you need to lay down to be fully present today?

The story of my life

STEP 22

Quote from *The Last Laugh*

Everything changes when you're told you only have five months to live, and you realise there's no time to wait. I've been speaking these words and challenging those I meet to think about what they'd do differently if they only had five months to live.

Pause for thought

My experiences and life lessons have left me wanting to share the goodness of God with everyone I meet. It would be such a waste for good not to come out of this bad experience.

It led me to write *The Last Laugh* (still available, by the way), and then go through the emotional roller-coaster of turning it into an audiobook. In preparation, I looked through family pictures, peeled onions and watched a few episodes of *The Repair Show* to try to get the tears out, but they still flowed freely in the recording studio.

We ended up with a pretty powerful resource. Who knew that onions and reality TV could be such potent tools for literary success?

 ## Steve's Story

When you share your story, amazing things can happen. I received a Facebook DM from a guy called Shaquille in Phuket City, Thailand, shortly after *The Last Laugh* was released. He explained, 'I work in the factory that printed your book, and I personally printed the covers. I also bought a copy for my nan, who's currently battling terminal leukaemia, and she's read it and found some great inspiration in it.'

God never fails to surprise me, but even I was astounded to receive this feedback from someone I had never met, who lives more than 6,000 miles away. It just goes to show that when we share our stories and spread inspiration, we can touch lives anywhere — whether it's someone in our own street or halfway across the globe.

Reflecting on ancient wisdom

You yourselves are our letter, written on our hearts, known and read by everyone. You show that you are a letter from Christ, the result of our ministry, written not with ink but with the Spirit of the living God, not on tablets of stone but on tablets of human hearts.'

(2 Corinthians 3:2-3)

 **Bekah adds:**

A friend came to see me last summer to ask for my advice. She's supporting a woman at church who is battling cancer, and was struggling to know how to help her. I shared what we had learned about asking someone what they need from us today, and she found it incredibly helpful. Our stories don't have to be miraculous or mind-blowing, but things we learn along the way can be useful for other people, too.

Something to think about

What have you learned about God, about choosing joy and about living well?

What good news do you have that might benefit others?

Is there anyone you know who might need a little encouragement or some of your wisdom?

Pray for an opportunity and for the discernment to know what and when to say something.

Time to say goodbye

As we turn these final pages, I can't help reflecting on the journey we've been on together. From the moment you first opened this book, you'll have realised this is far more than just a collection of simple steps to follow or a nice self-help guide. It's about holding firmly to faith while choosing to embrace joy, one day at a time. This is even more of a bonus if you happen to be named Joy and like hugs.

Through tears and laughter, setbacks and triumphs, and a whole lot of very mundane in-betweens, Bekah and I have learned invaluable lessons about building resilience, the importance of gratitude, and the transformative nature of laughter. Critically, we've learned that these are only truly possible when we choose to spend each day walking with Jesus, finding our strength, peace and security in the knowledge that he walks with us, and that we have a home in his unshakeable kingdom.

As you continue on your own path, remember that whatever life throws at you, you can choose your response.

Trust me, most days that choice is way harder than just deciding what to have in your Subway sandwich. When you look for it you'll discover joy can be found, usually in the most unexpected places. In Subway it'll probably take the form of a White Chip Macadamia Nut Cookie, free with your sub. Joy is often just lurking around the corner, waiting to surprise you. We pray you'll find it, embrace it, treasure it and spread it far and wide.

None of us knows what tomorrow holds, so let's continue to make the most of today.

Enjoy the adventure.

Live full lives, full in the fullness of God.

(Ephesians 3:19, MSG)

OTHER BOOKS BY STEVE LEGG

Making Friends: Evangelism the easy way
Man, Myth or Maybe More
Big Questions
The A-Z of Evangelism
Firm Foundations
The A-Z of Christmas
The Chancer
Paper Thongs and Further Misadventures
The Last Laugh

BOOKS STEVE WROTE WITH ALEXA TEWKESBURY

It's a Boy!
Lions, Whales and Thrilling Tales
The Lying Tree
cyberSky

BOOKS STEVE WROTE WITH BEKAH LEGG

All Together
Life Together
Time Together
Growing Together
Advent Together

"How long have I got, Doc? Five days? Five weeks? Five months? Five years?" "More like months," the oncologist replied.

When he heard this devasting news, Steve and his wife Bekah made a bold decision - they would get busy living and get busy laughing. Yes, there were tears that day and in those that followed, but Steve is a funnyman and a man of faith. He was never going to give cancer the last laugh.

'A journey of courage, faith, family and never giving up! I admire Steve so much.' – BEAR GRYLLS

THE LAST LAUGH

Reflections of a funnyman with terminal cancer

STEVE LEGG

'I couldn't put it down – laughing, brushing away a tear and going on a journey with Steve, the funnyman as he faced the no-joke reality of the diagnosis of a terminal illness. But this is not just Steve's story; he draws lessons that can change not only the way we view our death – but also our life.'

Rob Parsons OBE, author of *The Heart of Success*

Available at

amazon

or scan below

scm

Printed in Great Britain
by Amazon